IN THE BEGINNING
THERE WAS
No Sky

WRITTEN BY

Walter Wangerin, Jr.

ILLUSTRATED BY

Lee Steadman

Augsburg
MINNEAPOLIS

For my friends
Tom, Beth, Jill, and Kate—
the children who live down the lane from me.

IN THE BEGINNING THERE WAS NO SKY

Text copyright © 1997 Walter Wangerin, Jr.
Illustrations copyright © 1997 Lee Steadman

Published in association with the literary agency of Alive Communications, 1465 Kelly Johnson Blvd., Suite 320, Colorado Springs, CO 80920.

Cover and interior design by Elizabeth Boyce

Library of Congress Cataloging-in-Publication Data

Wangerin, Walter.
    In the beginning there was no sky / written by Walter Wangerin, Jr. ; illustrated by Lee Steadman.
      p. cm.
    Summary: A parent tells a child a personalized version of how God created the world.
      ISBN 0-8066-2839-1 (alk. paper)
    1. Creation—Juvenile literature. [1. Creation.] I. Steadman, Lee (Lee M.), ill. II. Title.
  BS651.W24 1997   97-28111
  231.7'65—dc21   CIP
                                                             AC

The paper used in this publication meets the minimum requirements of American National Standard for Information Sciences—Permanence of Paper for Printed Library Materials, ANSI Z329.48-1984. ∞

Manufactured in the U.S.A.   AF 9-2839
01   00   99   98   97   1   2   3   4   5   6   7   8   9   10

Child, come close to me. Come by me here, so that I can tell you a story.

There are two reasons for my story.

The first reason is that I love you.

And the second is that I saw you crying when you didn't know that I could see you.

Were you sad? I don't want my child to be sad. Were you hurt? People cry when they get hurt, don't they?

Were you lonely?

Well, when I saw you crying, I thought, *I know a story to make my dear one glad again.*

It's a wonderful story, child. You can think about it whenever you feel like crying again. And it's a true story. Perhaps you will start to remember the ending, even before I finish telling it to you.

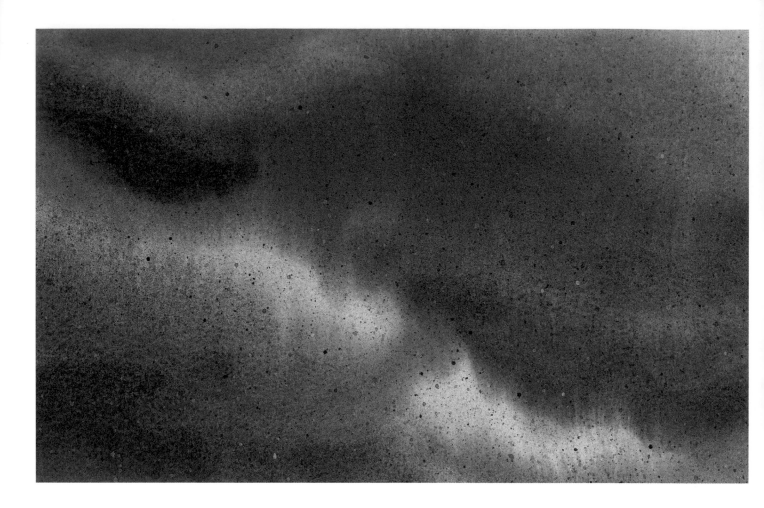

Once upon a time there was no sky. Do you know what that means, for there to be no sky? It's like a nightmare where bad things fly out of the blackness to get you. No roof on a house, no sky on the world! What could protect you then?

But God knew that.

God said, "I'm going to make a child." God said, "I'm going to love that child with all my heart. Nothing, nothing should be able to hurt or scare my beautiful child!"

So God climbed to the highest of high. And God, who is never afraid, cried out like thunder: "Let there be a hard thing, a firm thing, a *firm-mament* like a huge roof between the evil above and all the space below!"

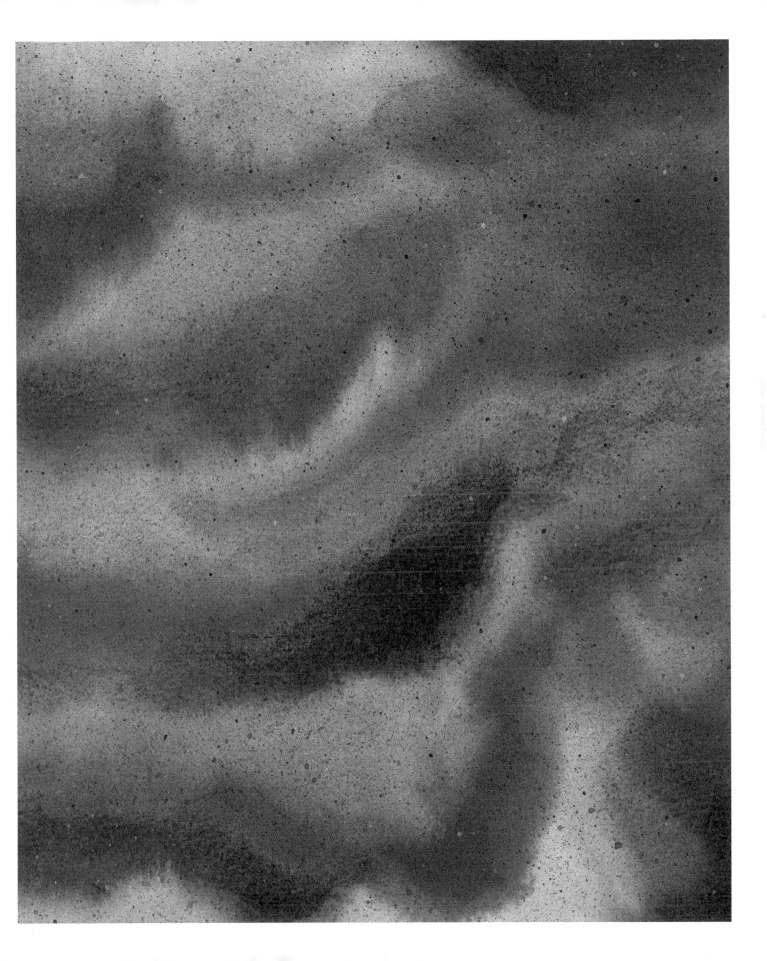

And right away the sky was there exactly as it is today: protection, child! A beautiful blue roof over all the world.

God blew it full of wind and cloud, and "Yes," he said. And "Good," he said. "It's just the way I want it to be."

But when he looked down, all God saw was water. There was nothing in the world but water, waves and waves and a deep green sea.

My little child, how long can you swim?

What? Can't you swim for a whole day long?

Well, God knew that.

God said, "I'm going to make a child. I'm going to love this child. And I do not want my child to drown or die!"

Oh, you should have seen what God did then.

Down came the Lord God Almighty with two big feet. He stomped in the water. He splashed and kicked and drove it backward, roaring, "Get to your shores! Get to your borders, you oceans and seas! Come down, you waters, in rivers and streams, and stay where I tell you to stay!"

So water poured down from the mountaintops, flashing like lizards in sunlight! Water ran to ponds and puddles, to pools and lagoons and lakes. Water rushed over the cliffs and fell into the sea, and the dry land appeared, places for children to stand or walk or sit or sleep, and the Lord said, "Yes! Good. I'll call the dry land Earth."

So God was glad.

But when he looked around, all he saw was sand. And stone. And a
bare black ground.

"But I'm going to make a child," said the Lord, "with a mouth and
a swallow—and you know that a tummy is sure to get hungry."

Tell me, my dear one: what do you like to eat?

God made it.

God made cherries and apples and peaches and plums, melons and pumpkins and berries and nuts—then beets and broccoli too. Even if you don't like them, God made them, because God knows what is good and very good for you.

So the earth was green and sweeter than roses, as soft as the grass, as warm as the morning, as bright as the day.

And did I mention that God hung lights in the sky? One for day and one for night. That's how the seasons got started.

But when all this was done, the Lord was frowning.

"I'm going to make a child, and I'm going to love my child," he said.
"But how would someone feel to be all alone in the world? Lonely! No,
it is not right that my child should be lonely. I will make creatures with
faces and voices! Yes, I will make friends for my child!"

So the Lord God thought up a marvelous, magical word. He went to the waters in rivers and seas, and he uttered the new word: *"Swarm!"* he said. The Lord said, *"Swarm!"*

Right away the waters began to bubble. They rippled and churned, and little fishes poked out their noses, and trout and bass and catfish swam, and salmon and sharks and swordfish—and way out in the ocean the great blue whale leaped over the waves, looking, looking around the whole horizon.

"God!" cried the blue whale. "God, I don't see it. Where is it?"

But God was high in the sky now, and God was whispering the magical word to the air: *"Swarm! Swarm!"*

And the wind seemed to wrinkle, and out of the wrinkles flew flocks of birds: sparrows and starlings and robins and cardinals and wrens and owls and ducks and swans and the powerful hawk—the hawk with yellow eyes, the hawk that can see grassblades from higher than the clouds: that hawk was frowning.

"God," cried the hawk. "God, where is it?"

But God was busy pulling creatures out of the ground, four-legged creatures, tiny mice and massive moose, beasts with claws and fangs and hoofs and paws, squirrels and weasels and sheep and dogs and cats and wolves and the grizzly bear.

"God," said the bear. She was up on her hind legs, peering everywhere with tiny eyes. "God," she bellowed, "where is it?"

God said, "Where is what?"

"The child!" said the bear,

"The child!" said the hawk.

"The child!" cried the blue whale out in the ocean. "Where is the little child who will lead us?"

God said, "I haven't made a child yet."

Oh, what a wailing there was then. All the animals howled together. They peeped, they shrieked, and they growled and grunted. They barked and brayed and cackled.

"You *have* to make the child," they cried. "Or who will tell us what our names are?"

"Well," said the Lord God Almighty. "Well, well," said the great Creator, "then it's time. Here are friends and food and the good earth and the blue sky, and the sun and the moon for telling the time. Yes, it is time, now—time to make my child."

So God walked down to a river valley.

All of the animals followed.

God strolled the banks of the river, looking for the very best clay.

The animals sat on the walls of the valley, hunched forward, watching.

Finally the Lord God found the perfect clay. He knelt down. He patted the clay together, forming a wonderful lump. Out of one side he pulled an arm; out of the other, another. He divided the lower portion into two legs, then the dear Lord leaned down and with the tips of his fingers began to carve a beautiful face: two eyes, both of them closed; two ears as cold as seashells; a little mouth; a nose with holes, but no air going in and no air coming out.

Then God paused, gazing down, his fingers on the beautiful cheek below him. And the animals grew restless.

"Is that all?" they called. "God, that child is as cold as stone!"

There was a tongue in the mouth, but the tongue couldn't move. There were lungs in the chest, but they were empty. There was a heart, but it was only a clay heart, silent and still.

Suddenly the animals saw something else, and they grew nervous.

"What's the matter with God?" they whispered. "Is he sad? Is he hurt?"

They saw that the great Creator was crying.

Tears were falling from his eyes upon the face of his clay-child, and God was washing that face with his hands and his tears, so that there were two faces shining the same kind of light, one above the other.

No, God was not sad. Neither was he hurt.

God was crying because he loved this child so much. He was weeping for joy at the birth of a beautiful person.

And then God did what he had never done before.

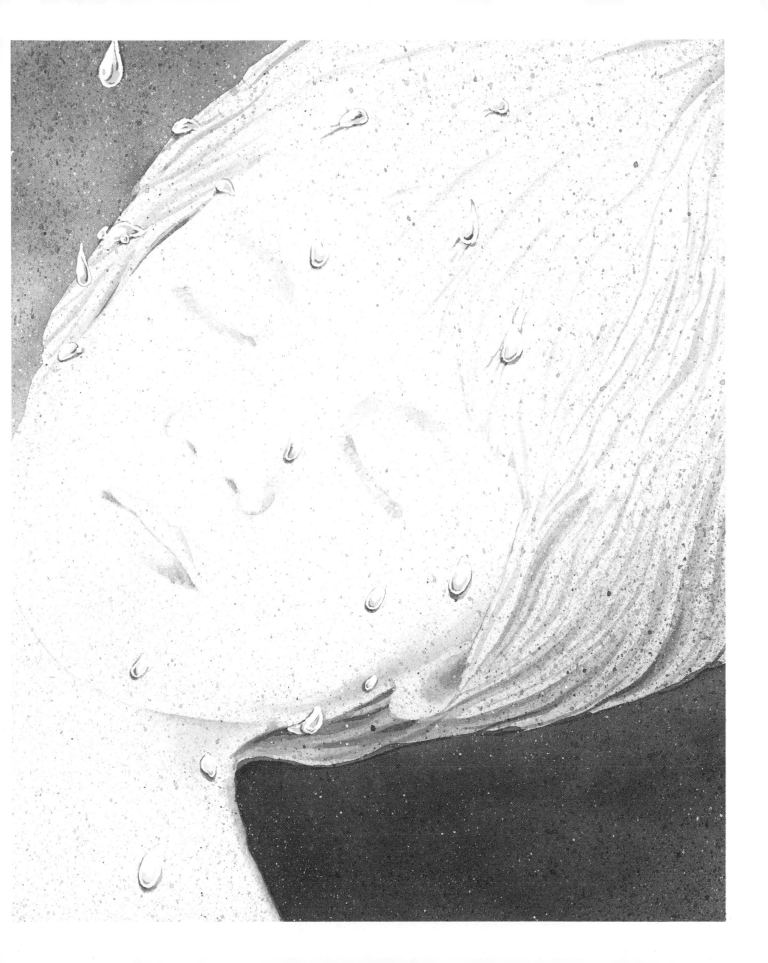

He bent down. Do you remember this part, child? He leaned down closer and closer to the mouth below, till the lips and the lips were touching.

Do you remember? You should.

Because then the dear God kissed you.

And while he was kissing you, he breathed out. And you breathed in. God breathed his own breath into your lungs, so they began to blow up like little balloons. And then, *boom:* your heart began to beat. Do you remember? Oh, the blood flowed out to your hands and your feet, and they felt warm and soft and strong. And then you sucked in your own big breath—remember? You ought to remember.

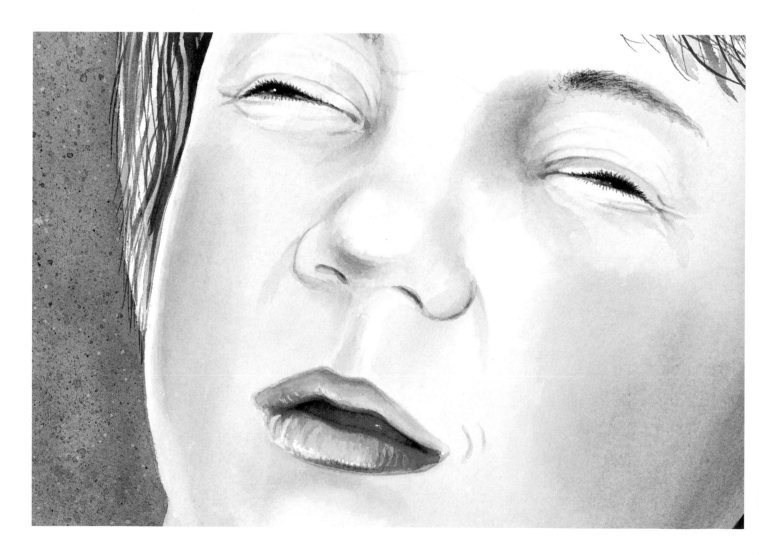

Because what you did with your breath was, you sneezed in the face of God Almighty!

God rocked backward.

And your eyes flew open, and you thought it was thundering. But that wasn't thunder at all. It was the roaring laughter of the Lord. He was laughing on account of the sneeze in his face.

Then all the animals joined in, giggling, roaring, bellowing, laughing.

And then God began to poke you in the ticklish places.

He poked you in your cheek, and he said, "Child, I put a tongue in there. Use it. Laugh and talk the live-long day, and tell your friends good things wherever you go."

He poked you in your arms and legs, and he said, "Child, I put speed and skill and strength in there. Walk in the joy of my green earth. Give the earth a good day's work, and it will give you food forever."

And finally—do you remember this?—he poked you in your chest, and the Lord God said, "Child, I put a heart in there. Love me. Love all the creatures I have made. Love everyone, dear little child, exactly as I love you now."

This is a true story. Tomorrow, go out and look at the world and see the truth of my tale: the sky, the green earth, all the living creatures. Then come inside and give me a hug.

Will you feel sad or hurt again? Perhaps. And perhaps I will one day tell you the story of why we feel such things.

But for now, remember my story. Remember that God cried too, but he cried for you because he loved you so much. He still does.